Teacher's Pet

By Katie Dale

Illustrated by Elif Balta Parks

Chapter 1

"Come on, Gizmo!" said Tom, picking up Gizmo's cage. "Today you're coming to school for Show and Tell! Are you excited?"

Gizmo didn't reply. After all, Gizmo was a hamster.

Plus, Gizmo was asleep. Hamsters always slept during the day. But he was still

'Teacher's Pet'
An original concept by Katie Dale

Illustrated by Elif Balta Parks

Published by MAVERICK ARTS PUBLISHING LTD

Studio 11, City Business Centre, 6 Brighton Road,

Horsham, West Sussex, RH13 5BB

+44 (0)1403 256941

A CIP catalogue record for this book is available at the British Library.

ISBN 978-1-84886-726-0

Maverick publishing

www.maverickbooks.co.uk

White

This book is rated as: White Band (Guided Reading)

very cute and fluffy and Tom couldn't wait to show him to everyone.

At school, everyone was showing the things they'd brought in. Anya had brought a huge ostrich egg and Krish was holding a knight's helmet. But as Tom walked in, everyone hurried over to peer into Gizmo's cage.

“Awesome!” Krish grinned.

“He's so cute!” Anya cooed.

Tom smiled. He knew everyone would love Gizmo.

Well, nearly everyone.

“What is that?” Mr Hanson said, walking into the classroom and pointing at the cage.

“This is Gizmo,” Tom said. “I brought him for Show and Tell.”

“Wait, is that a-a hamster?!” Mr Hanson's eyes widened and his nose twitched. “But I'm allergic to ha-a-atchoo!” He sneezed and sat down quickly. “Atchoo! ATCHOO! ATCHOOOO!”

“Oh no! Mr Hanson must be allergic to hamsters,” said Krish. “My mum's allergic to dogs. They make her sneeze too.”

“My uncle's allergic to bee stings,” added Anya. “He has to go to hospital if he gets stung.”

“Oh no!” said Tom. “Should we fetch the nurse?”

But before anyone could do anything, the strangest thing happened...

Mr Hanson stopped sneezing... and started snoring! He curled up on his chair, his eyes tightly closed.

"Mr Hanson?" Anya said quietly. "Are you asleep?"

"No I am not!" came a voice. But it wasn't Mr Hanson who spoke... it was Gizmo!

"Let me out of this cage!" Gizmo demanded. Everyone stared at the hamster.

"Gizmo?" Tom said slowly. "Did you just... talk?"

"I am not Gizmo!" the hamster squeaked. "I am your teacher, Mr Hanson!"

Chapter 2

"Oh my gosh! Mr Hanson must have swapped bodies with Gizmo!" Tom gasped. "That's why he's asleep! Hamsters are nocturnal!"

"But that's impossible!" argued Anya.

"So is a talking hamster!" said Krish.

"But how did you turn into a hamster, Mr Hanson?" Tom asked, opening the cage. He'd always thought his teacher was a bit hamster-like, with his big teeth and twitchy moustache, but he'd never actually turned into one before!

"I have a very rare allergy," the hamster sighed. "It runs in my family. Whenever I'm near hamsters, I turn into one!"

"We have to tell the headmistress!" Anya said.

"No!" Mr Hanson cried. "Please! You can't tell anyone! Not today of all days!" Fear shone in the hamster's beady black eyes. "Because today the school inspector's coming!"

“WHAT?” Everyone started to panic.

“The inspector can't see you like this!” Anya cried.

“We just need to wait,” Mr Hanson said.
“I always change back after a while.”

“But what if the inspector sees you before then?” Tom said.

“He'll close the school!” Krish wailed. “We can't have a hamster teacher!”

Everyone looked at each other hopelessly.

Suddenly, Anya smiled. “I have a plan.”

Chapter 3

The knock at the door made everyone jump.

"C-come in!" Mr Hanson called nervously.

The headmistress walked in with a man in a suit. "Inspector, this is Saturn Class and their teacher, Mr..." The headmistress froze as she looked at Mr Hanson.

He was sitting in his chair at the front of the classroom...

...wearing a knight's helmet.

“I'm Mr Hanson,” Mr Hanson said, from his hiding place behind the helmet. “Good morning, Inspector.”

Tom held his breath. Would they make Mr Hanson take his helmet off? Or notice that he wasn't moving at all?

“Today we're learning about medieval knights,” Mr Hanson explained quickly. “So I thought wearing a helmet would help bring the lesson to life.”

‘And hide the fact that Mr Hanson's talking without moving his lips!’ thought Tom nervously.

“Hm. Very inventive,” the inspector said, smiling. But then he frowned. “Why is that cage door open?” The inspector pointed at Gizmo's cage. “I hope there isn't an animal running around the school?

That would break several health and safety rules!"

Tom froze. Krish turned pale. Anya gulped.

"Of c-course not!" Mr Hanson stammered, thinking quickly. "I brought that cage ready for our n-new class pet, but it hasn't arrived yet."

"I see," the inspector said. "Good. Class pets are a wonderful idea. Keep up the good work!"

Everyone breathed a sigh of relief as the inspector and headmistress left the classroom.

"Well done, Anya!" Mr Hanson said, jumping onto the desk. "That was an excellent plan."

Anya beamed. “I'm just glad it worked, and we can all relax now!”

“Er...I think you spoke too soon,” said Krish. “Gizmo is waking up!”

Gizmo shook his head, knocking the helmet to the floor with a clatter. Then he jumped down from the chair and ran out of the classroom - on all fours!

“Stop him, quick!” Anya cried as everyone chased after him.

Chapter 4

As everyone chased after him, poor terrified Gizmo ran faster and faster down corridor after corridor, and then outside!

“Oh no!” Tom said. “What if he gets out of the school!”

"Double oh no!" Anya cried. "There's the inspector!"

Sure enough, the headmistress and inspector were staring at Mr Hanson as he ran across the school field on all fours, followed by his entire class.

"We have to stop Gizmo!" Tom yelled. "But how?"

"I've got an idea!" Krish said, running back inside.

Poor Gizmo ran all the way across the school field, then tried to scramble up the fence to get away. He was very confused that he couldn't climb it.

“Shh, Gizmo, it's okay,” Tom said, reaching out a hand to stroke him, but then he stopped.

Was it weird to stroke your teacher's back, even if he was actually a hamster?

“Here!” Krish said running over with a carrot. “Hamsters love carrots, right? Mum always gives me some in my lunch box.”

“Good thinking, Krish!” Tom handed the carrot to Gizmo, who immediately started nibbling it happily. Phew!

“Now we just need to get him back inside,” Anya said.

“What's going on over here?” said a voice. Tom froze. It was the inspector.

“Um, we always have a quick run between lessons,” Krish said quickly. “Mr Hanson says it's good for us to get fresh air.”

“Yes,” Anya said. “It keeps us fit and helps us focus.”

The inspector nodded. Then he frowned. “But what are you doing now, Mr Hanson?”

The teacher didn't reply. He was still nibbling his carrot.

“We're, er, having a drama class,” Tom said quickly. “We have to guess what animal Mr Hanson is pretending to be. He can't talk because he's in character.”

"And animals can't talk," Krish said. "Usually."

Tom glared at him.

The inspector looked at Mr Hanson. "Well he's clearly pretending to be a hamster."

"Of course!" Anya said. "Well done, inspector! Now we all have to pretend to be hamsters too!"

Immediately the children all started nibbling and scratching, pretending to be hamsters.

"Um, let me show you the rest of the school now," the headmistress said quickly, leading the inspector away.

As soon as they were out of sight, everyone sighed with relief.

“Thank goodness that's over!” Mr Hanson said.

“Mr Hanson! You've changed back!” Anya cried. “Phew!”

“Phew indeed!” Mr Hanson said, smiling. “But what happened with the inspector? How on earth did you explain why I was running around on all fours?”

“Krish and Tom told him we were keeping fit then doing a drama class!” Anya said.

“How clever!” Mr Hanson smiled. “Thank you all.

Your quick-thinking has saved my job, and probably saved the school!"

Everyone beamed.

But then Tom frowned. "But if you're Mr Hanson, where on earth is Gizmo?"

"Gizmo must still be in the classroom, where I was before I changed back!" Mr Hanson said.

"We have to find him before the inspector sees him!" Anya cried. "You heard what he said - having a wild animal running around breaks loads of health and safety rules!"

"I'll get more carrots!" Krish cried.

Chapter 5

Everyone searched the classroom for Gizmo.

They looked under desks, on top of cupboards, behind the radiators, but there was no sign of him anywhere.

"Gizmo!" everyone called. "Gizmo, where are you?"

"He could be anywhere!" Tom said anxiously. "We'll never find him!"

“And if the inspector sees him, all our hard work today will be for nothing!” Anya sighed.

“Tom!” Mr Hanson said suddenly. “Look!” He covered his nose and mouth with his handkerchief and pointed at the cage.

“Gizmo! Thank goodness!” Tom said, locking the cage quickly.

“Phew! It's finally over!” Anya grinned.

Suddenly there was a knock on the door and the inspector walked in. Everyone froze. What now?

“I just wanted to congratulate you, Mr Hanson,” the inspector said. “I've been very impressed with the enthusiasm and creativity you put into your teaching.”

"Well, I have a great class," Mr Hanson said, smiling at everyone. "They inspire me."

Everyone beamed.

"Oh, and I see your class pet has arrived!" The inspector smiled, peering into the cage. "What is it? A *rat*? No... Oh no..." He turned pale and started backing away. "Is that a... a..."

"That's Gizmo," Tom said nervously. "My hamster."

"Oh thank goodness!" the inspector said. "I thought it was a gerbil. I'm allergic to gerbils!"

Everyone laughed.

The End

Book Bands for Guided Reading

The Institute of Education book banding system is a scale of colours that reflects the various levels of reading difficulty. The bands are assigned by taking into account the content, the language style, the layout and phonics. Word, phrase and sentence level work is also taken into consideration.

Maverick Early Readers are a bright, attractive range of books covering the pink to white bands. All of these books have been book banded for guided reading to the industry standard and edited by a leading educational consultant.

To view the whole Maverick Readers scheme, visit our website at
www.maverickearlyreaders.com

Or scan the QR code above to view our scheme instantly!